From the Roots

GUIDED POETRY JOURNAL

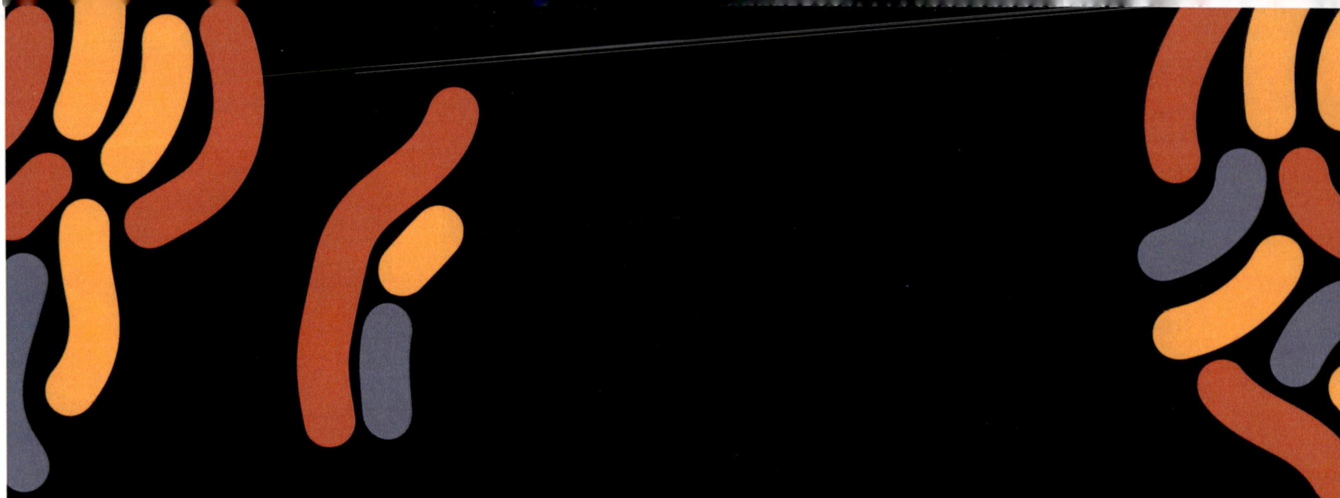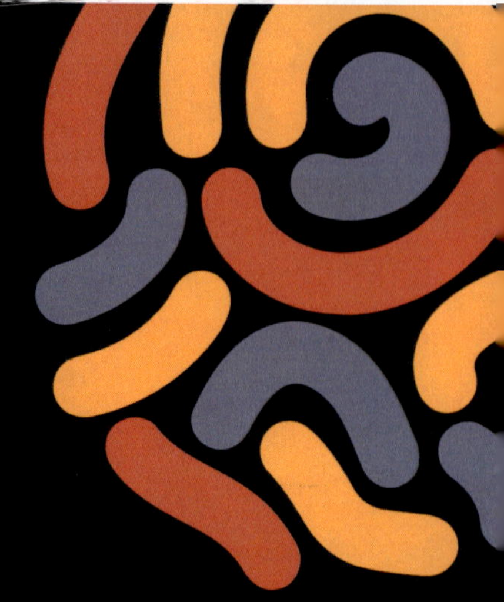

WE INVITE YOU TO STAY CONNECTED AND BE A PART OF OU COMMUNITY. JOIN US ON THIS INCREDIBLE JOURNEY AS WE CONTINUE TO CREATE MAGICAL MOMENTS AND SPREAD POSITIVITY THROUGHOUT OUR COMMUNITY.

FOLLOW US ON SOCIAL MEDIA @HOCARTISTS TO RECEIVE THE LATEST UPDATES AND BEHIND-THE-SCENES SNEAK PEEKS.

TOGETHER, WE CAN MAKE A REAL CHANGE. YOUR CONTINUED SUPPORT MEANS THE WORLD TO US. THANK YOU FOR BEING AN ESSENTIAL PART OF OUR MISSION.

CONTACT@HOCARTISTS.COM

#MAKINGARTMATTER

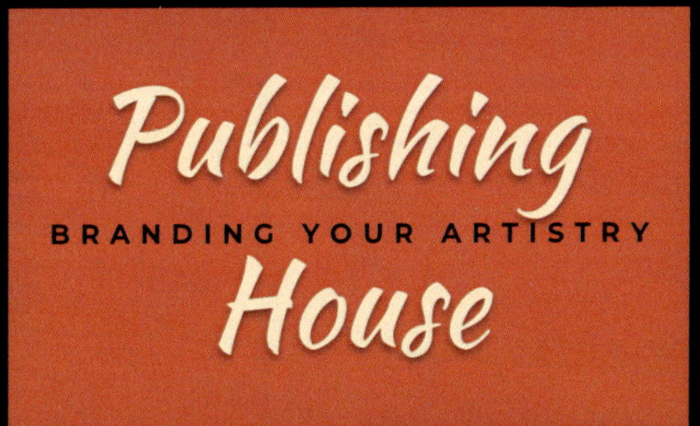

Branding Your Artistry Publishing House

From The Roots: Guided Poetry Journal

First Edition

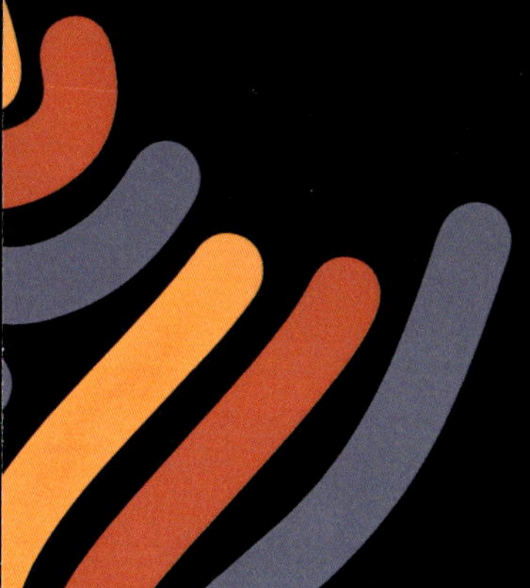
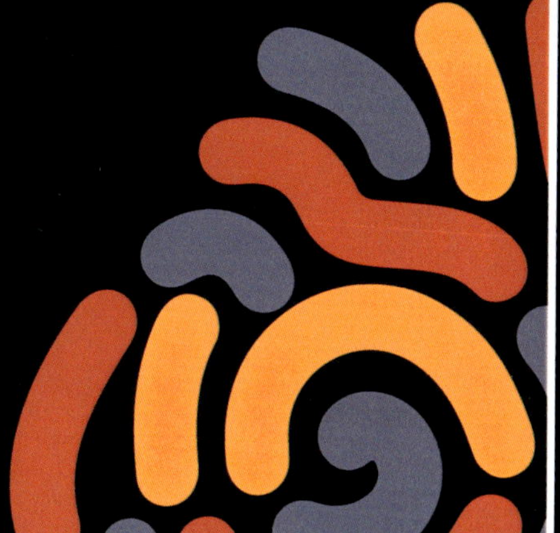

Table of Contents

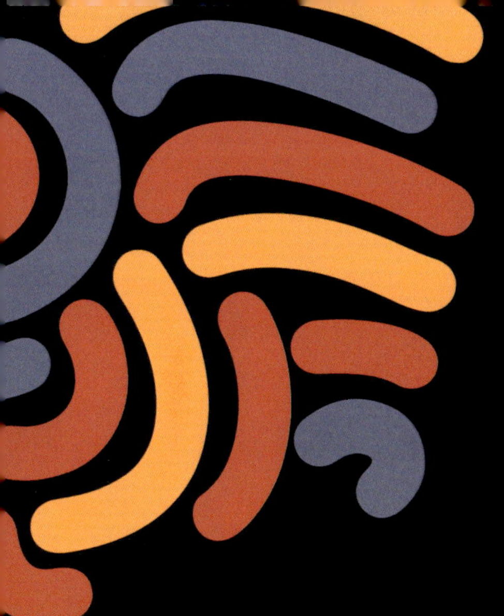

This Journal Belongs To:

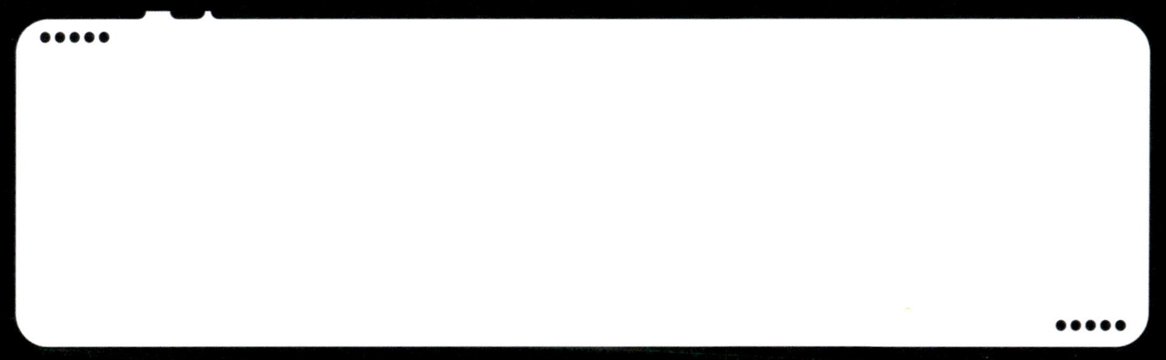

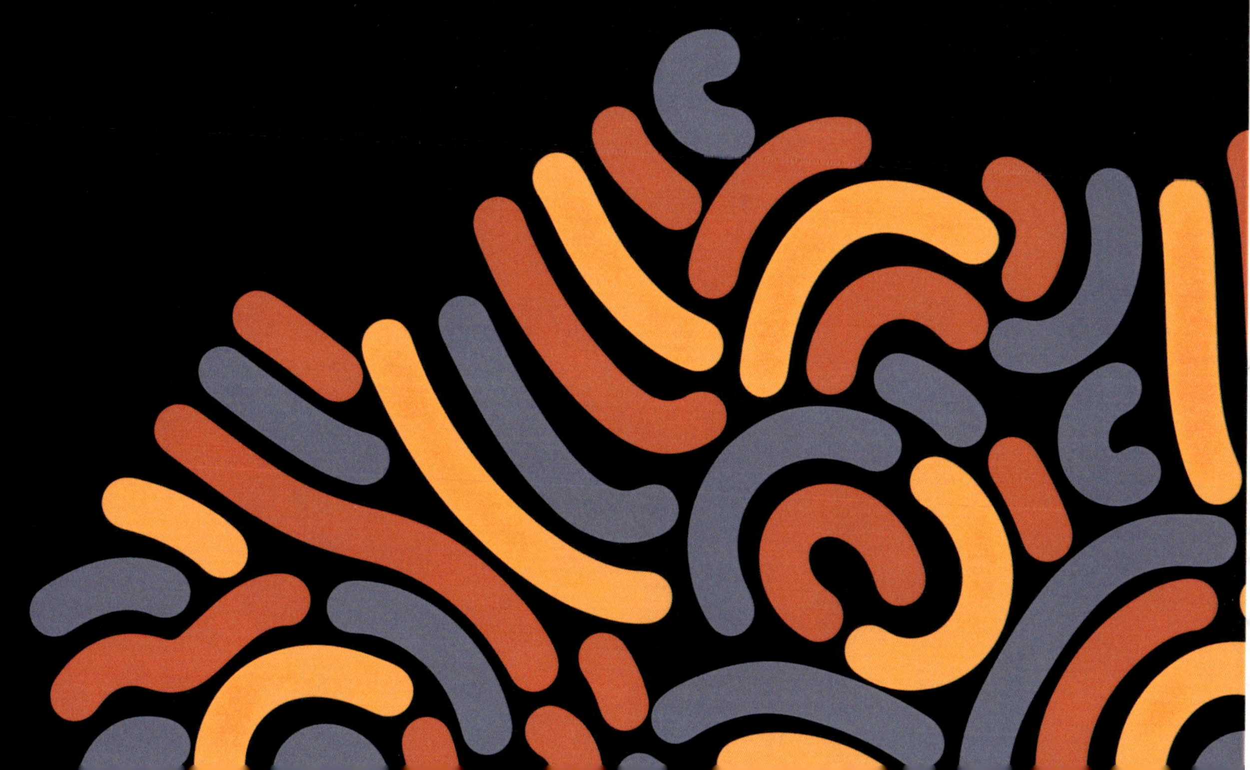

PART I

Warm Up prompts

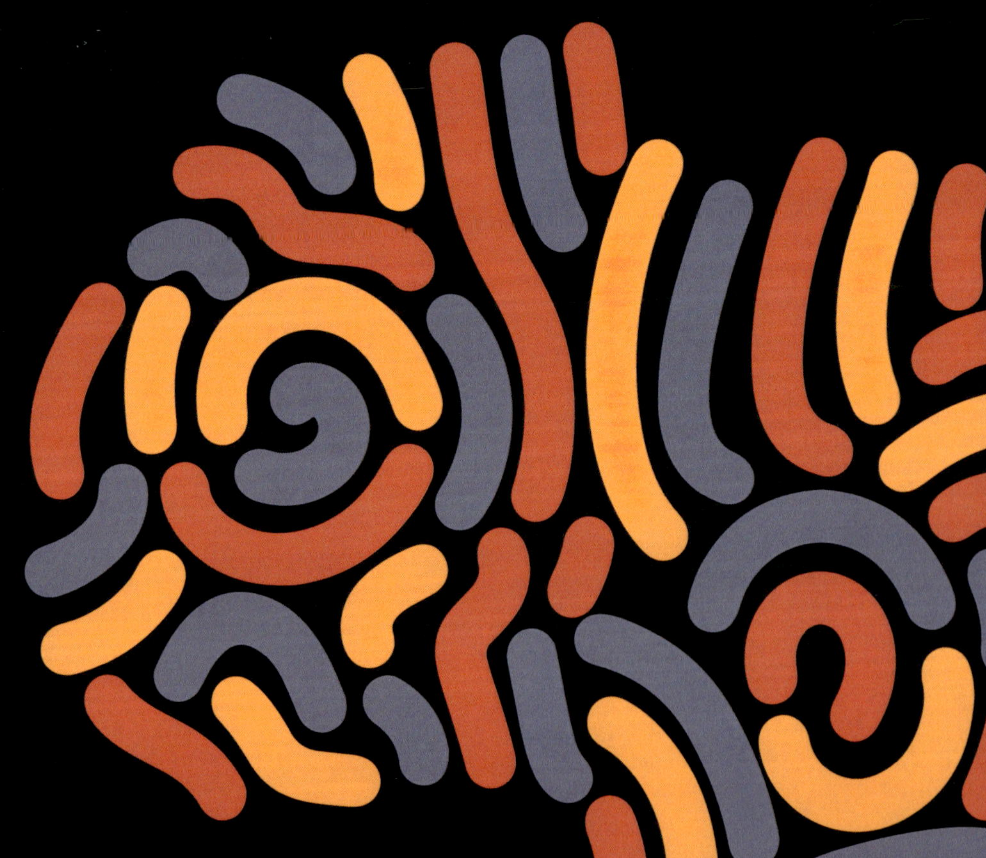

GETTING ACQUAINTED

Welcome to the realm of warm-up prompts designed to spark connection and familiarity. This collection of thoughtful exercises invites you to embark on a journey of getting acquainted, both with yourself and with others. Through these prompts, you'll delve into self-reflection, engage in meaningful conversations, and explore various aspects of your identity. Whether you're seeking to deepen your understanding of your own desires, values, and aspirations or to foster meaningful connections with new acquaintances, these warm-up prompts will serve as a springboard for self-discovery and genuine connections. Get ready to dive in, open up, and embrace the magic of these prompts as you embark on a journey of self-exploration and interpersonal connections.

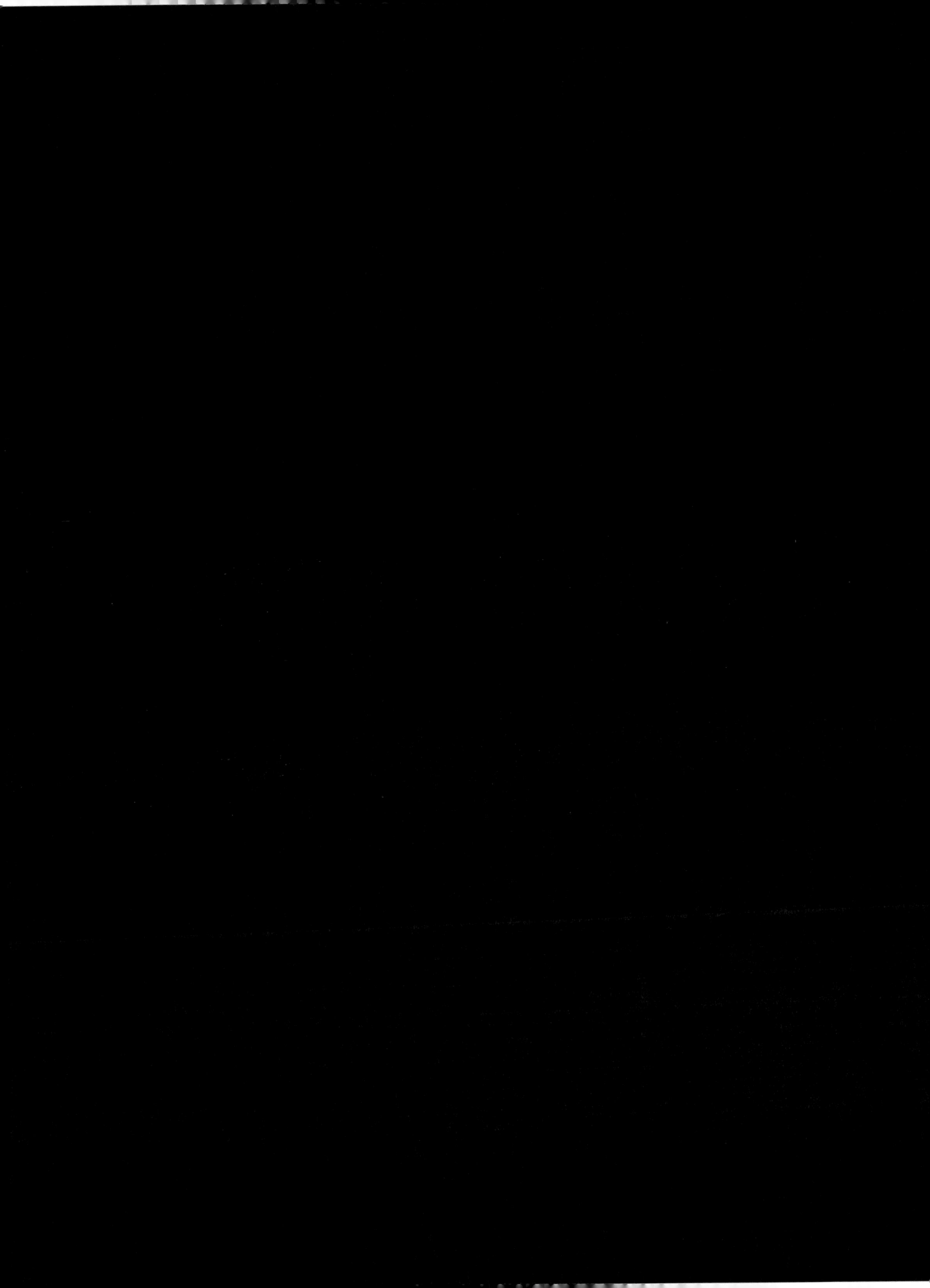

<u>Date :</u>

write about a time when you where truly happy

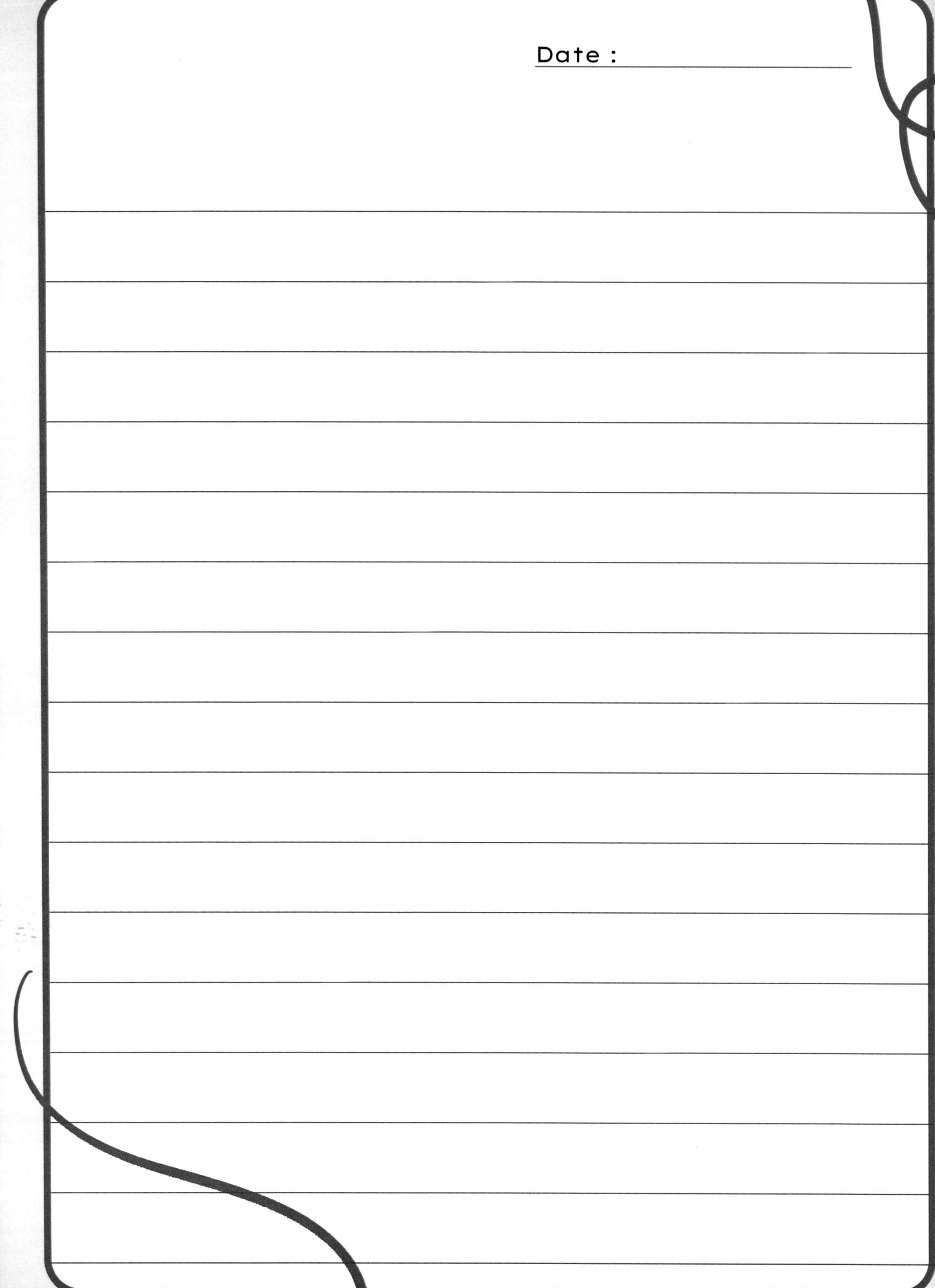
Date :

Create a simple list of things you use every day,
starting with the ones that are most important to you.

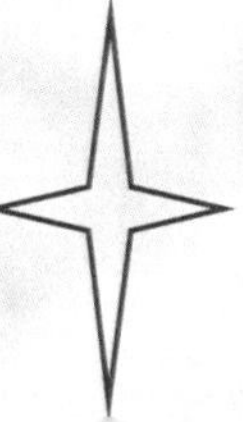

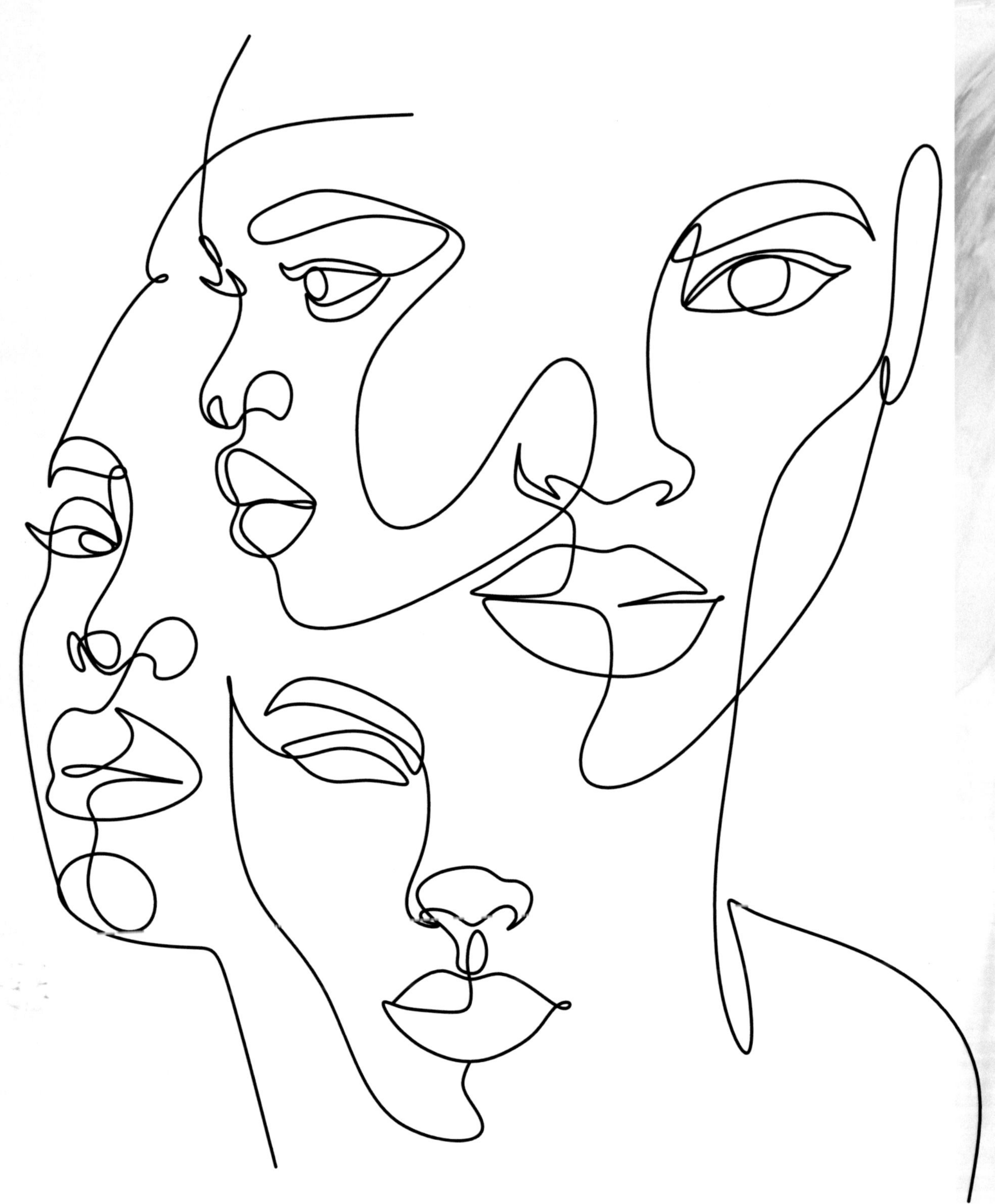

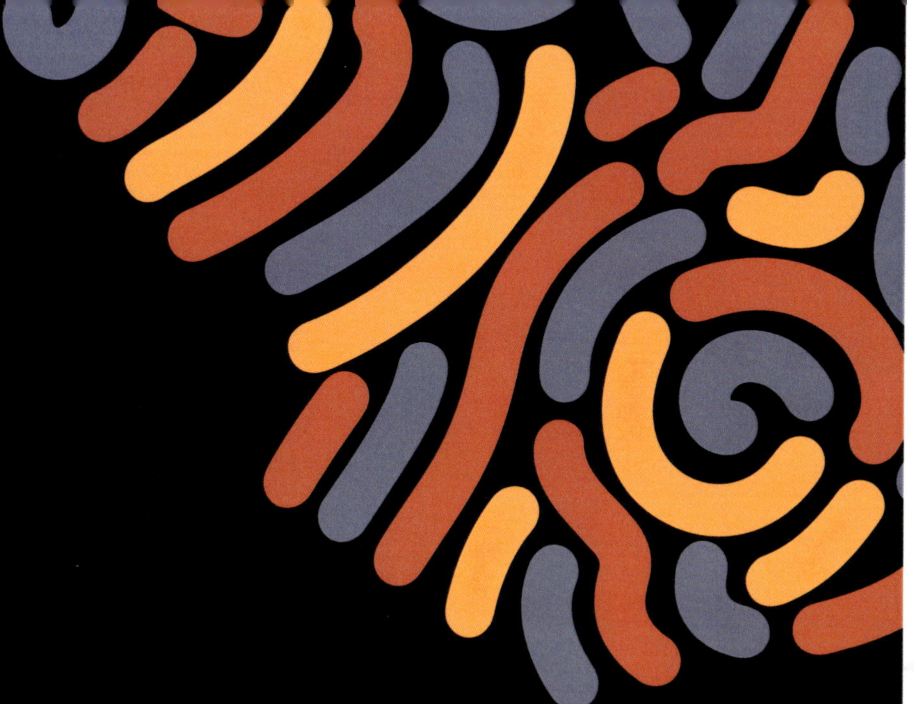

Poetry is the
rhythmical creation
of beauty in words.

EDGAR ALLAN POE

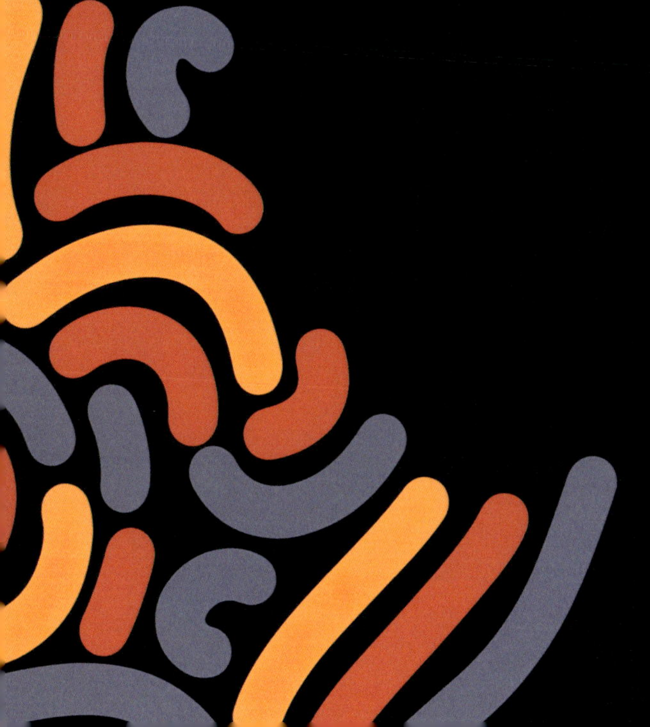

Which states have you traveled to? And where would
you like to go on your next exciting adventure?

Describe the places you liked the most and disliked the most from the list of states you've visited. Think about the locations that made you feel happy and those that you didn't enjoy as much. Write about what you loved and what you didn't like.

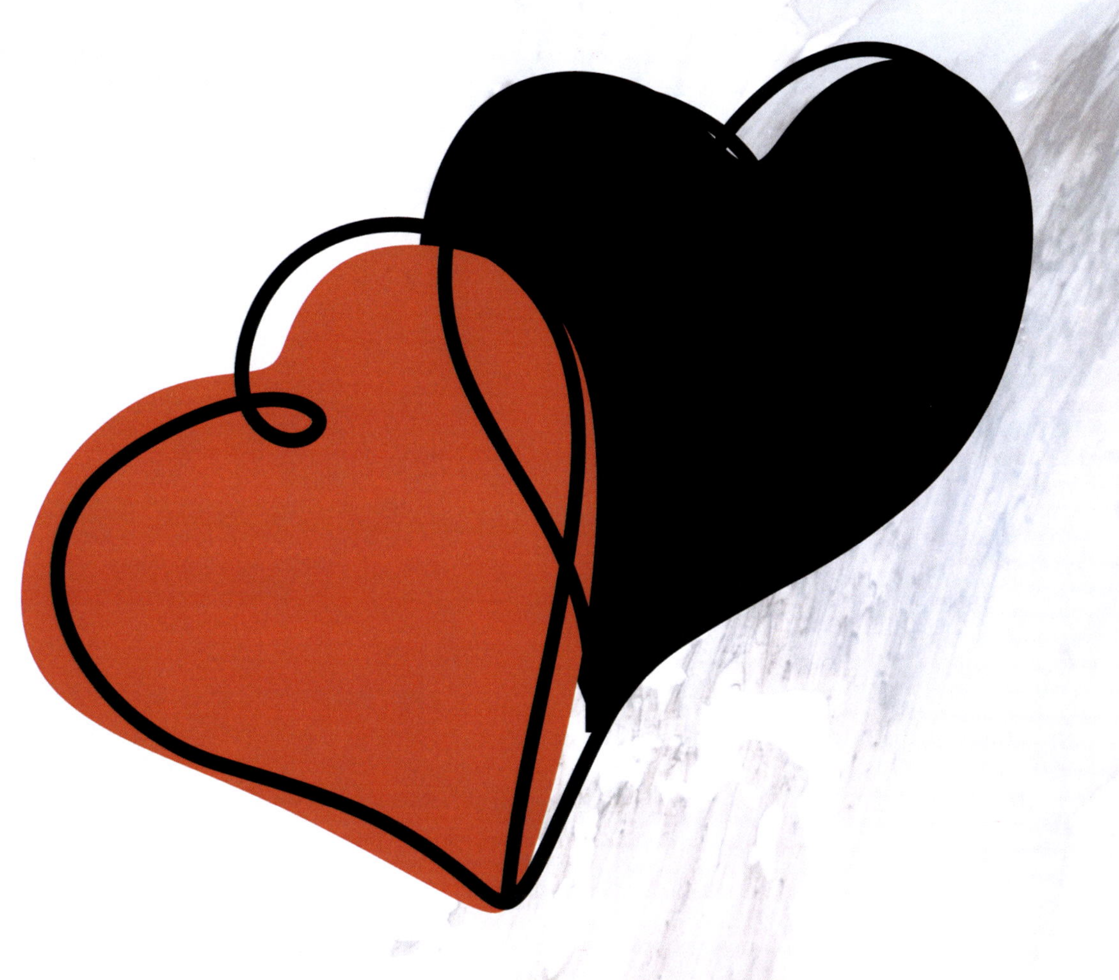

love yourself

Write about something you healed from and the steps you took to heal

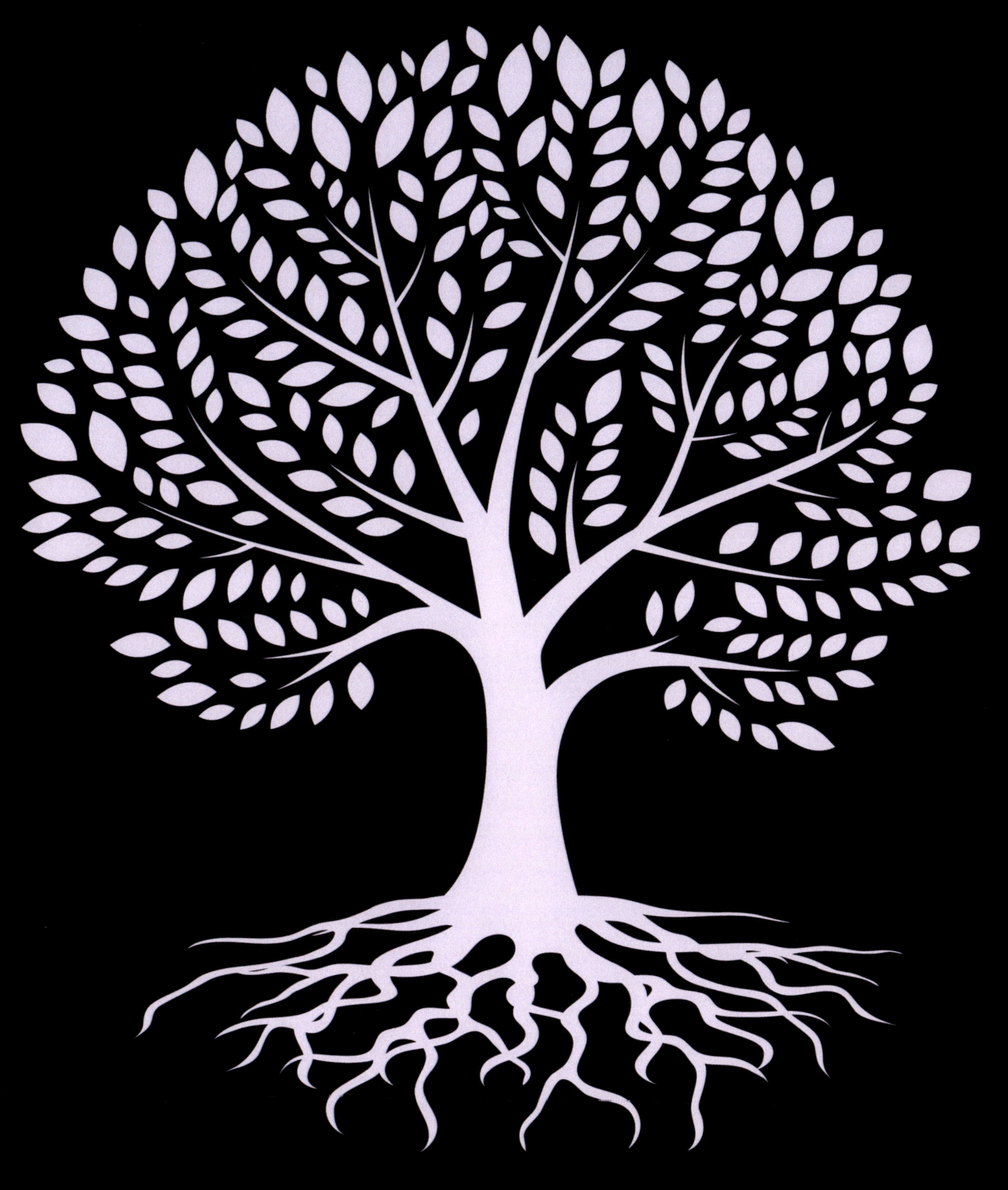

Family Tree

Reflect upon a significant moment you shared with your family, one that holds deep meaning. Consider the emotions, connections, and experiences that unfolded during that time.

ALLITERATION

A literary device characterized by the repetition of consonant sounds at the beginning of nearby words in a phrase or sentence. It is used to create a musical or rhythmic effect, enhance the flow of language, and emphasize certain words or ideas. Alliteration adds a touch of melody and artistry to written or spoken language, capturing the listener's attention and enhancing the overall aesthetic appeal of the text. It is commonly used in poetry, prose, slogans, and advertising to create memorable and engaging phrases. By repeating consonant sounds, alliteration can evoke emotions, create vivid imagery, and heighten the impact of the words being used.

EXAMPLES:

- "Silent as shadows, the shimmering sea"
- "Whispering willows weep in the wind"
- "Dancing daffodils in delightful display"
- "Misty morning meadow, murmuring melodies"
- "Serenading stars sprinkle silver secrets"

In these examples, the repetition of consonant sounds adds a lyrical quality to the phrases, creating a musical and rhythmic effect. The alliteration enhances the imagery and helps to evoke a specific mood or atmosphere in the reader's mind.

Compose a comprehensive list of alliteration phrases and mark the ones that resonate with you or that you want to incorporate into a poem.

Write a heartfelt note of gratitude thanking your present self.

Date : _______________________

Write a heartfelt note of gratitude thanking your former self.

thank you

Write a poem about your favorite Hobby

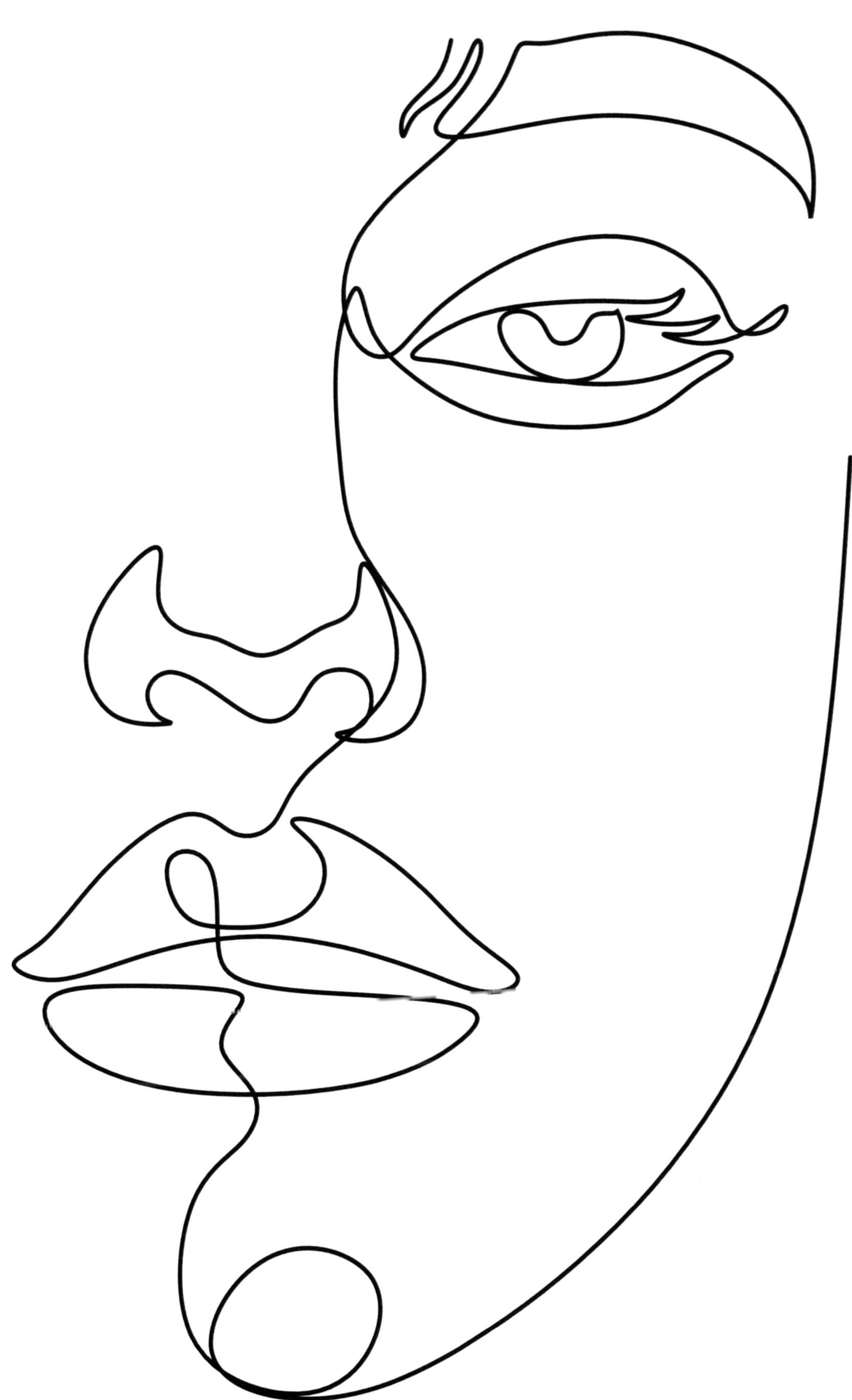

Write a poem inspired by the hues of a color

Date : ___________________

Write a poem about something that happened this week

Reflect on a valuable lesson you have recently learned and explore its significance through your writing.

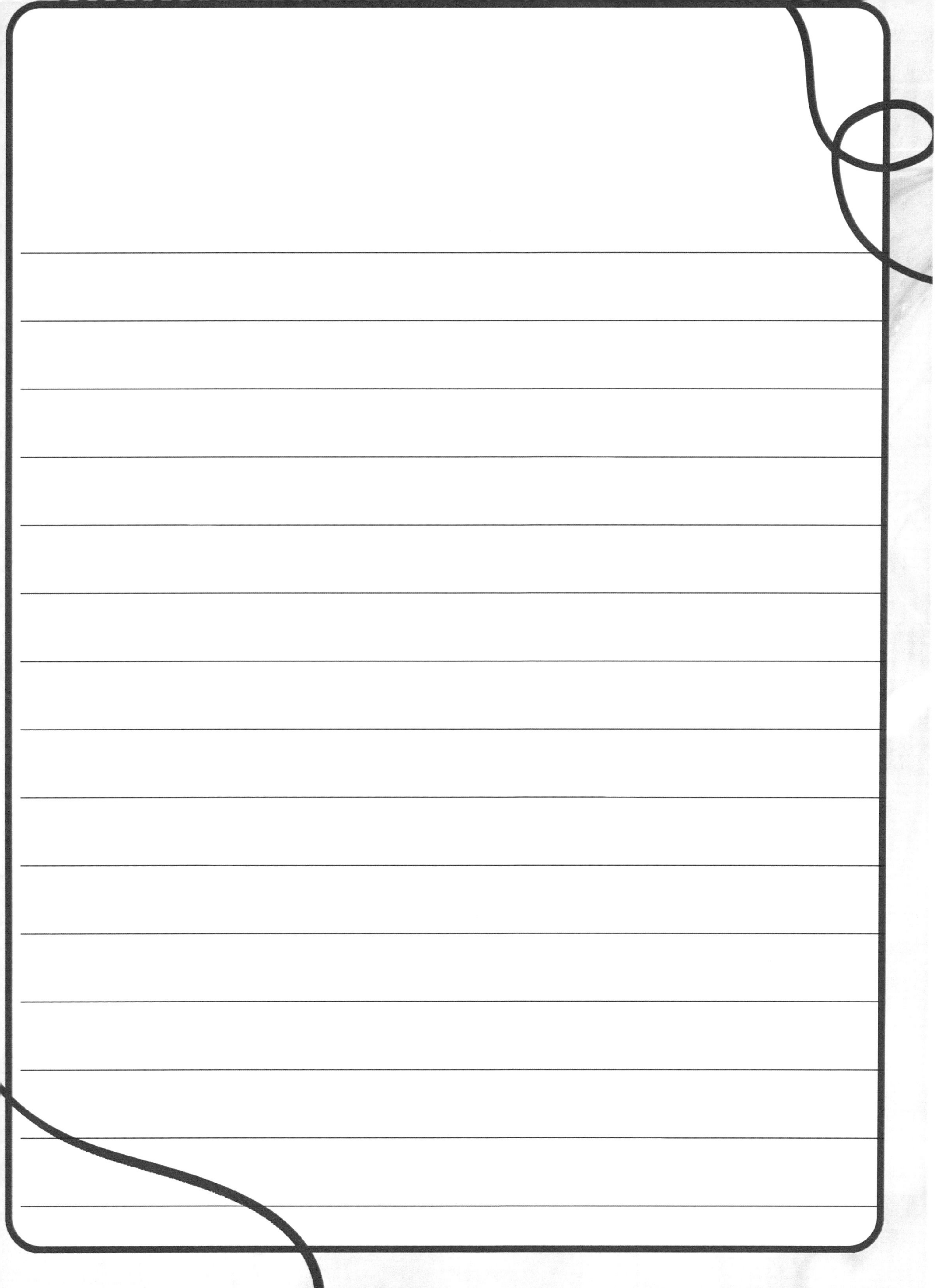

IDIOM

A phrase or expression that has a figurative meaning different from the literal interpretation of its individual words. It is a unique form of language that is specific to a particular culture or language group. Idioms are used to convey a deeper, often symbolic or metaphorical message, and they add color, creativity, and richness to our communication. They may be rooted in historical, cultural, or social contexts and are commonly used in everyday conversations, literature, and other forms of artistic expression. Understanding idioms requires familiarity with their intended meanings and usage, as they cannot be deciphered by simply examining their individual words.

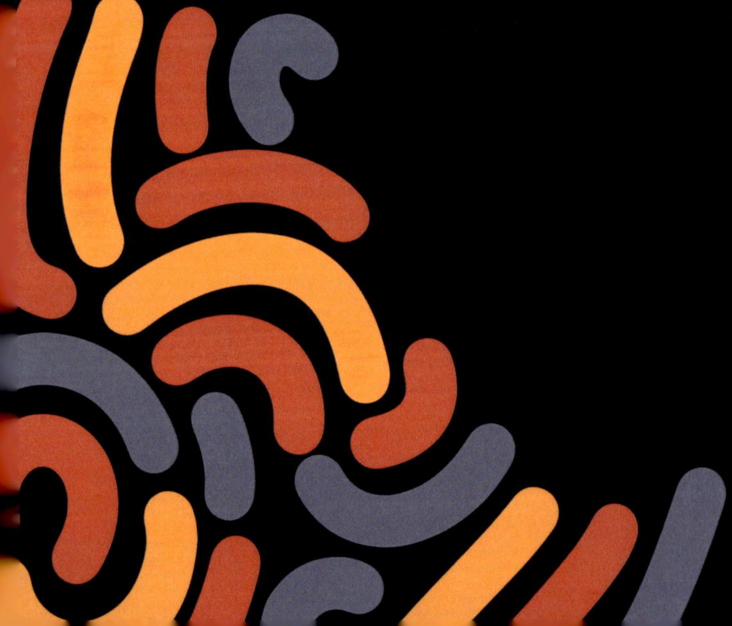

EXAMPLES:

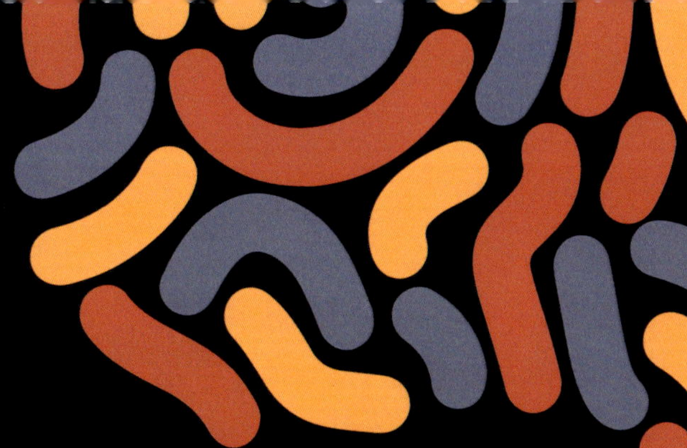

"Break a leg" - To wish someone good luck, especially before a performance. It means to do well or succeed.

"Bite the bullet" - To face a difficult or unpleasant situation with courage and determination.

"Hit the nail on the head" - Describes someone who accurately identifies or addresses a problem or issue.

"Kick the bucket" - A euphemism for dying or passing away.

"Piece of cake" - Something is very easy or effortless to do.

"Cost an arm and a leg" - To describe something that is very expensive.

"Break the ice" - To initiate or facilitate a conversation or social interaction in order to make people feel more comfortable.

"Barking up the wrong tree" - To someone who is pursuing the wrong course of action or making a false assumption.

"In hot water" - To be in trouble or facing a difficult situation.

"Let the cat out of the bag" - To reveal a secret or disclose information that was meant to be kept confidential.

Explore a cherished childhood toy, movie, book, or any other nostalgic artifact, and connect it to the present day, delving into the enduring significance it holds in your life.

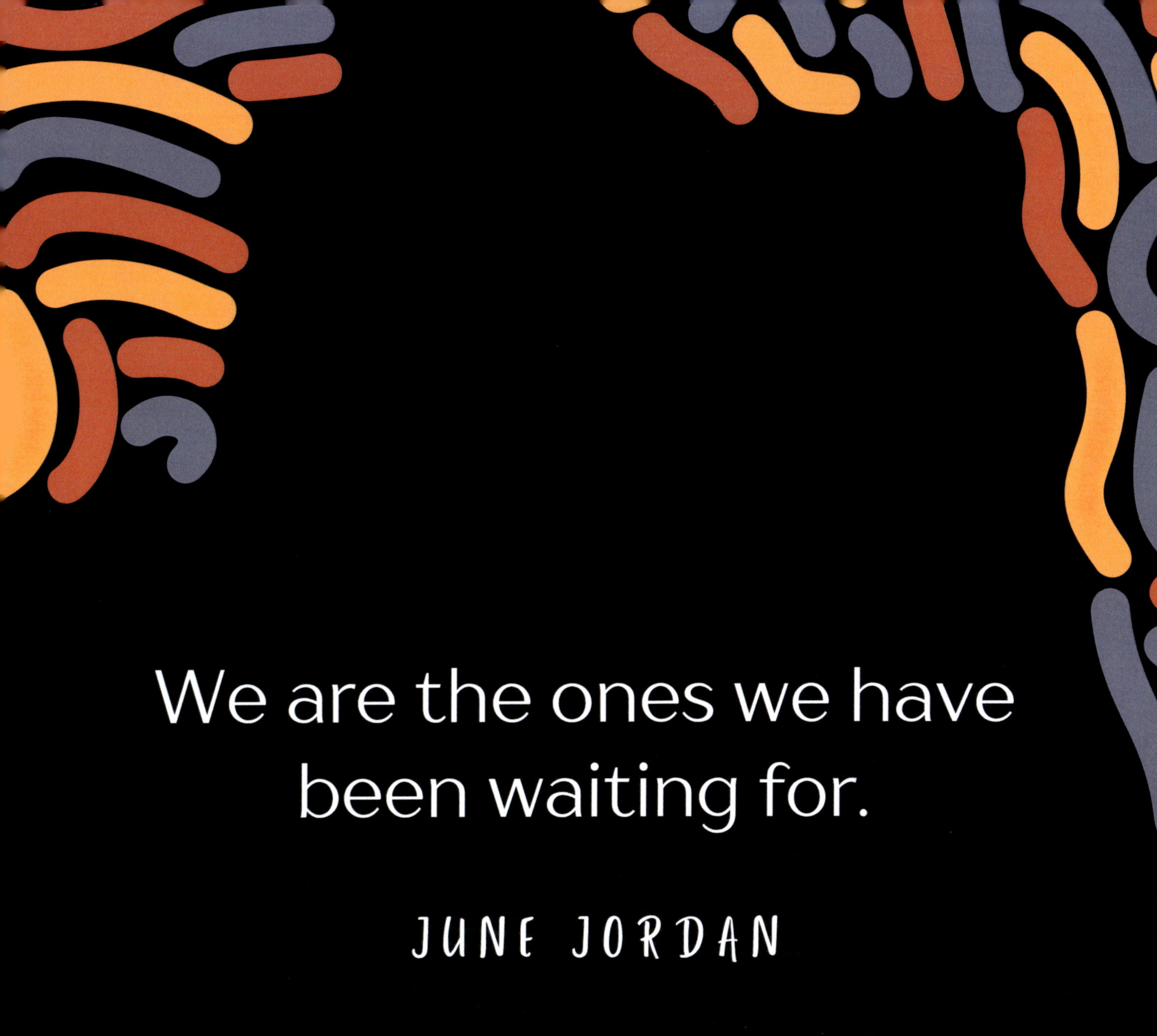

We are the ones we have been waiting for.

JUNE JORDAN

IF YOU COULD FREEZE TIME IN ONE MOMENT OF YOUR LIFE, WHAT WOULD IT BE? WRITE A POEM IN HONOR OF THAT MEMORY

Unleash your creative flow by crafting a poem without lifting your pen from the paper, starting from the inspiration of your favorite vegetable.

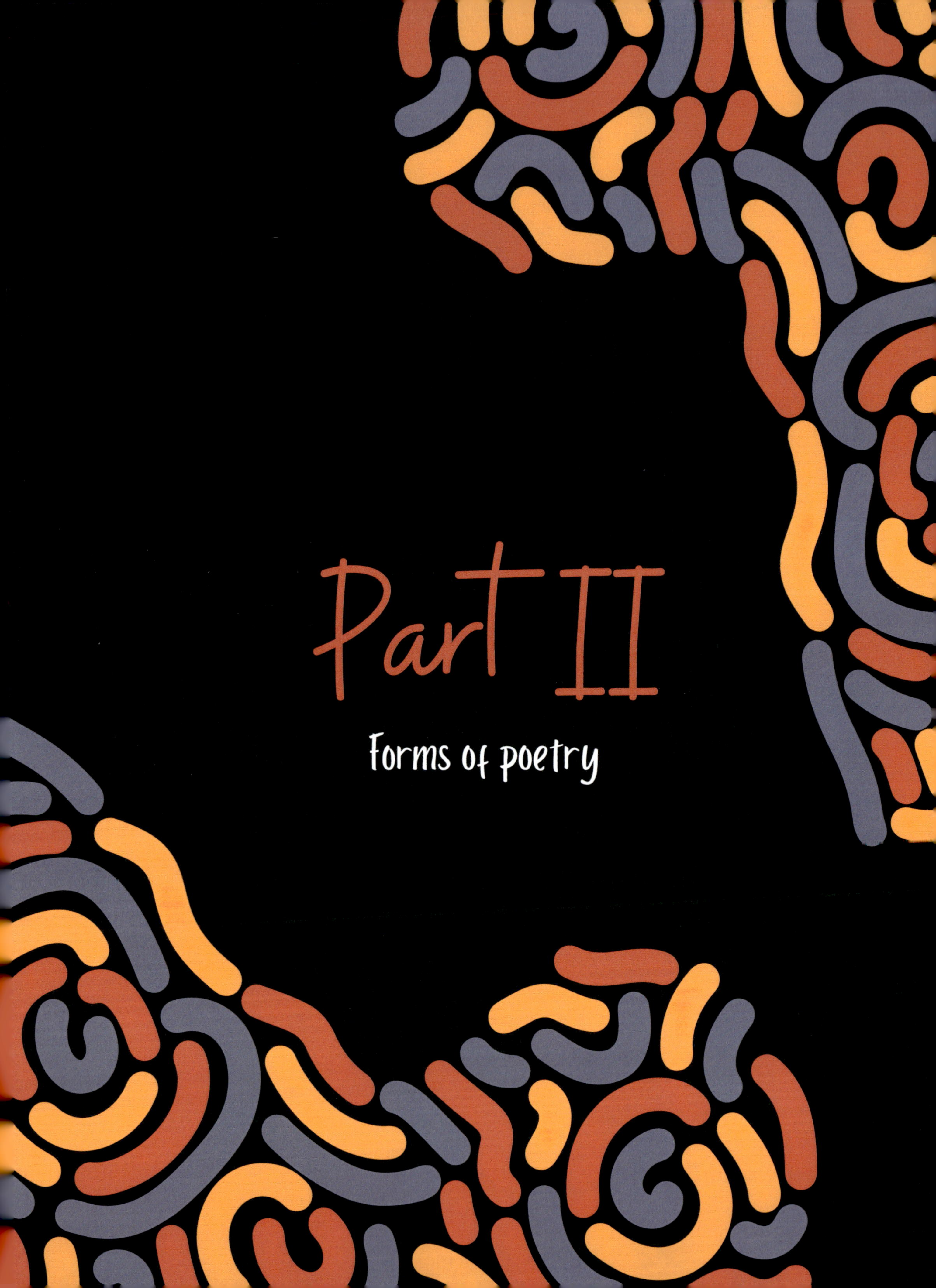

Part II

Forms of poetry

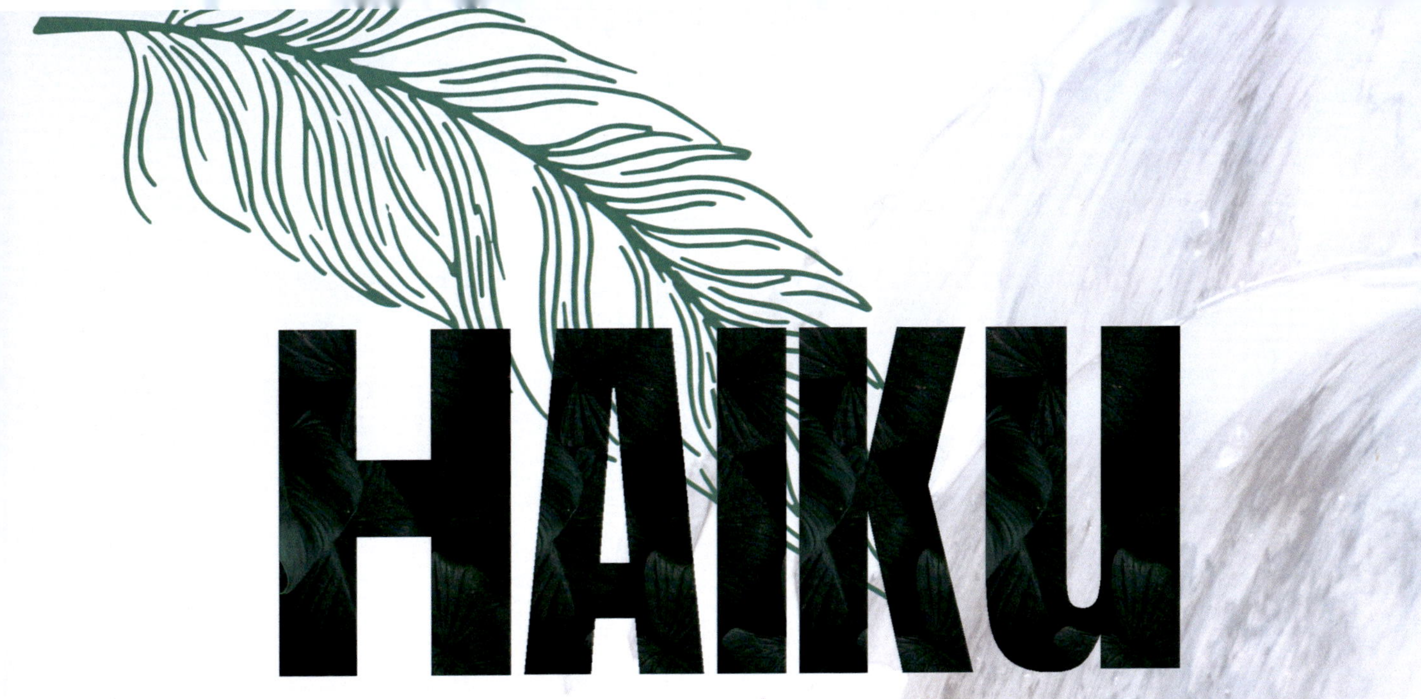

HAIKU

A captivating form of Japanese poetry, invites you to embark on a journey of expression. Composed of just seventeen syllables artfully arranged in three lines of five, seven, and five syllables respectively, haiku has a profound ability to evoke vivid images of the natural world. Rooted in tradition, this poetic form captures the essence of nature's beauty and invites you to immerse yourself in its serene and fleeting moments. Explore the art of haiku, as you skillfully craft your own verses and bring to life the captivating landscapes that surround us.

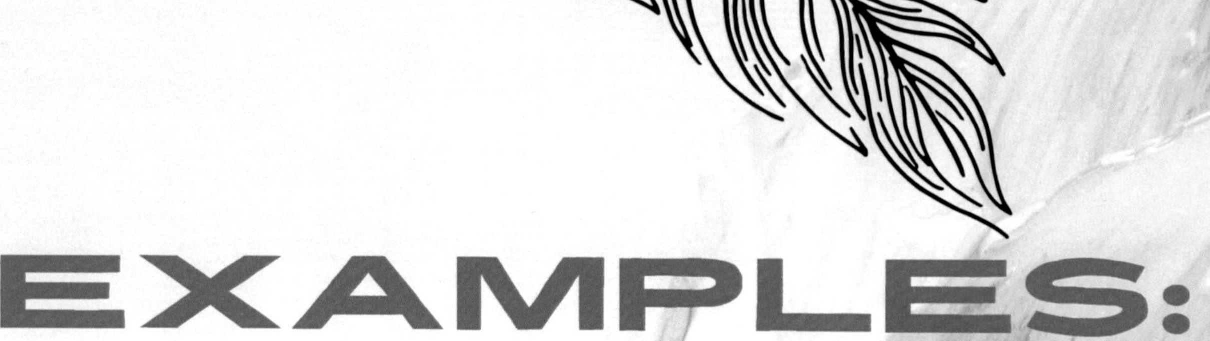

EXAMPLES:

"An old silent pond" - Matsuo Basho (5 syllables)
"A frog jumps into the pond— " (7 syllables)
"Splash! Silence again." (5 syllables)

"In the cicada's cry" - Kobayashi Issa (5 syllables)
"No sign can foretell" (7 syllables)
"Summer's end is near." (5 syllables)

"Over the wintry" - Matsuo Basho (5 syllables)
"Forest, winds howl in rage" (7 syllables)
"With no leaves to blow." (5 syllables)

"In the twilight rain" - Masaoka Shiki (5 syllables)
"These brilliant-hued hibiscus— " (7 syllables)
"A lovely sunset." (5 syllables)

Date :
Haiku This; Nonesense

Haiku This; I Am

Haiku This; I Am

Date :
Haiku This; inspiration

Haiku This; Hope

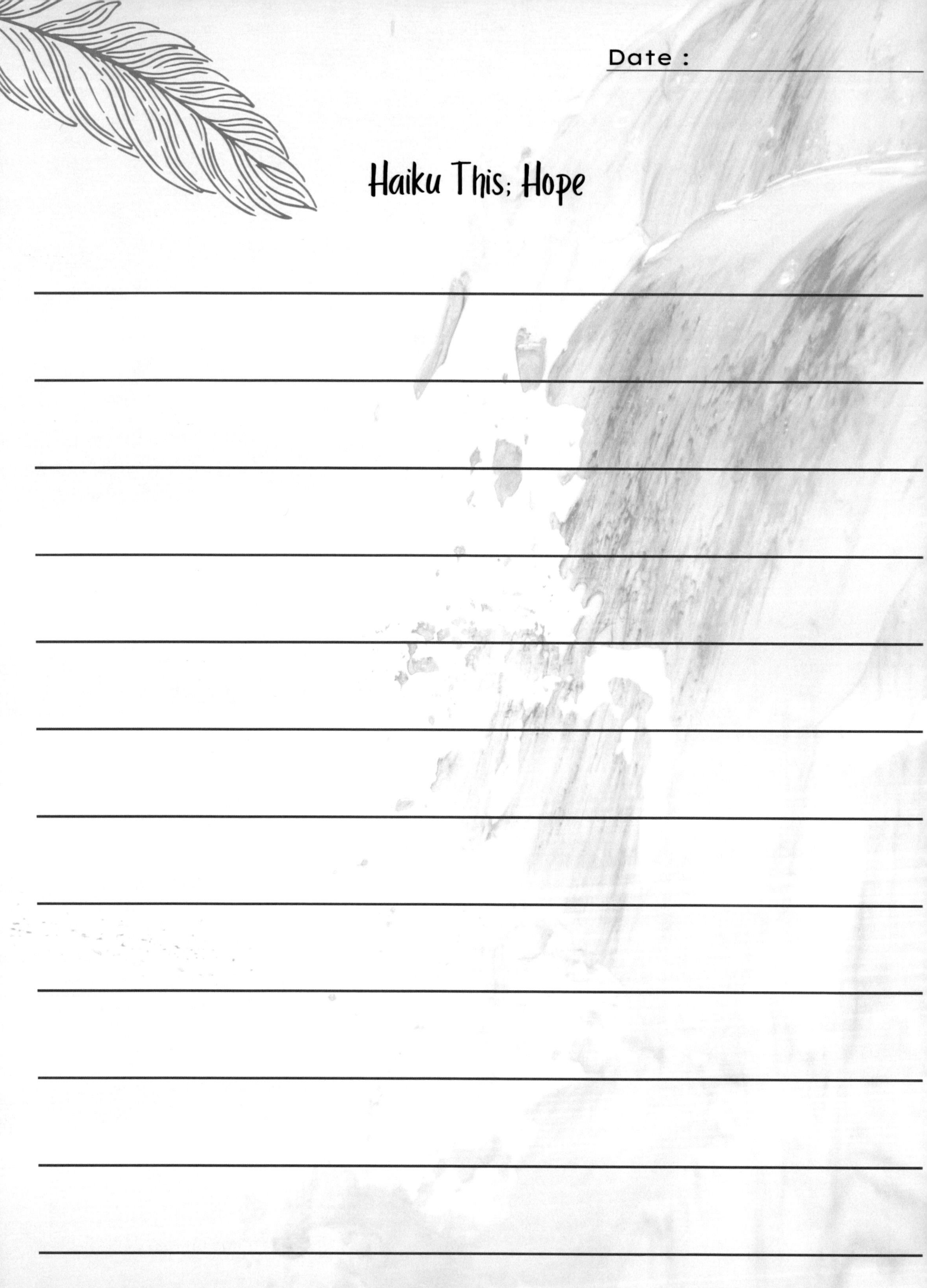

Date :

Haiku This; loyalty

Poetry is the rhythmical creation of beauty in words.

EDGAR ALLAN POE

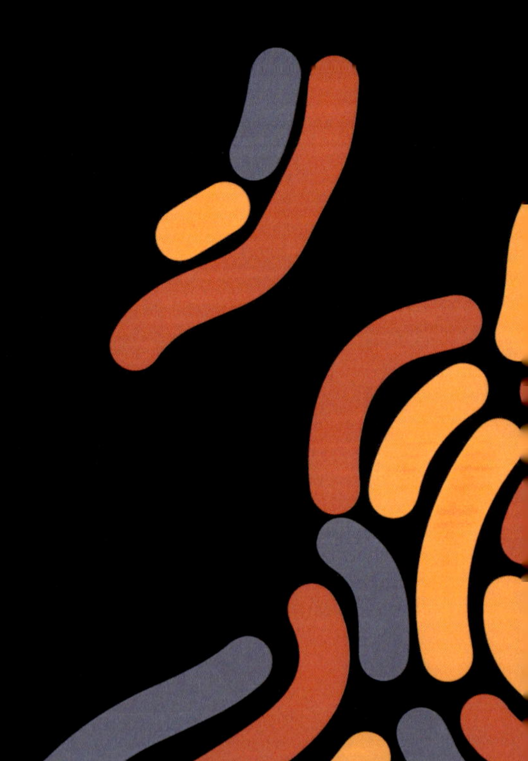

Acrostic

Discover the artistry of acrostic, a creative form of expression that combines poetry, word puzzles, and composition into a harmonious whole. In an acrostic, the enchantment lies in the arrangement of certain letters within each line, forming a word or even words when read vertically. This unique interplay of language unveils a hidden message, lending an intriguing layer of depth to your compositions. Unleash your imagination as you craft acrostic poems or dive into the world of word puzzles, unraveling the secret meanings concealed within each line. Embrace the challenge and delight in the fusion of words and creativity that acrostic offers, weaving a tapestry of linguistic ingenuity that is uniquely yours.

EXAMPLE:

Rise

Radiant spirits breaking the chains of the past
Inspiring hope with each step forward
Strength in our souls, resilience that lasts
Empowering voices, a legacy restored

Write an acrostic poem using the word
"fall" as the foundation for each line,

write an acrostic poem using your name

write an acrostic poem , using the word
"love" as the foundation for each line,

write an acrostic poem , using the word
"color" as the foundation for each line,

write an acrostic poem , using the word
"inspiration" as the foundation for each line,

Courage is the most important of all the virtues because without courage, you can't practice any other virtue consistently.

MAYA ANGELOU

BALLAD

A captivating form of verse that weaves a captivating narrative using poetic language and employs a specific rhyming pattern across its four stanzas. Through the artful use of lyrical phrases, it tells a tale that engages and enthralls the reader, creating a memorable and evocative experience.

EXAMPLE:

"The Rime of the Ancient Mariner"
by Samuel Taylor Coleridge:

It is an ancient Mariner,
And he stoppeth one of three.
'By thy long grey beard and glittering eye,
Now wherefore stopp'st thou me?

The Bridegroom's doors are opened wide,
And I am next of kin;
The guests are met, the feast is set:
May'st hear the merry din.'

He holds him with his skinny hand,
'There was a ship,' quoth he.
'Hold off! unhand me, grey-beard loon!'
Eftsoons his hand dropt he.

He holds him with his glittering eye—
The Wedding-Guest stood still,
And listens like a three years' child:
The Mariner hath his will.

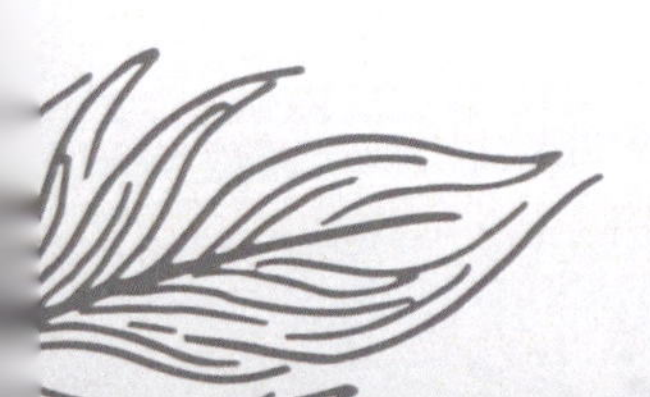

write a heartfelt ballad chronicling the transformative journey of an individual's healing, as they find solace and resilience through therapy and self-exploration.

write a ballad that tells the tale of an individual who finds peace through transformative power of forgiveness, whether they're giving or receiving it

Write a ballad about a love that is lost but
never forgotten.

Write a ballad about a tragic love story between two people from different social classes

Poetry is the spontaneous overflow of powerful feelings: it takes its origin from emotion recollected in tranquility.

WILLIAM WORDSWORTH

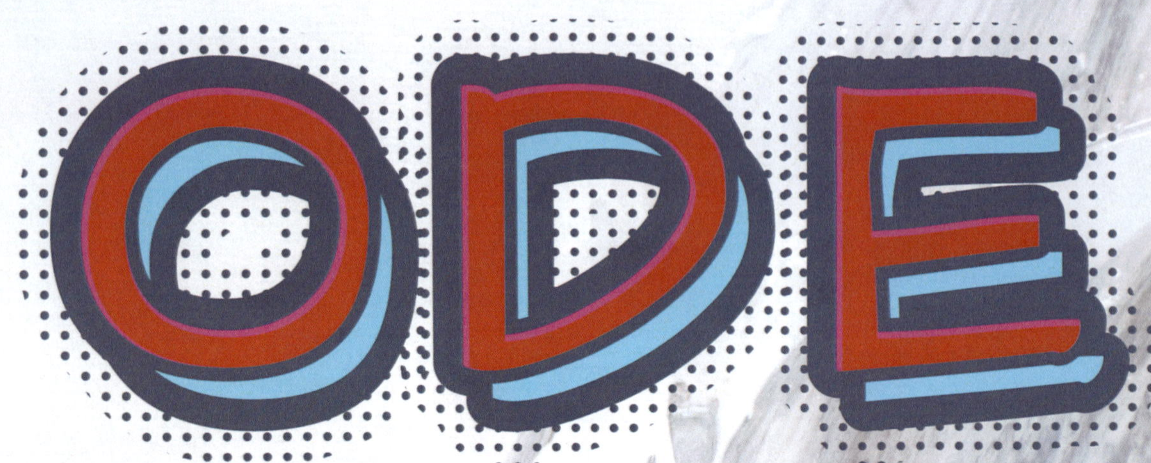

A poem that celebrates or praises a particular person, place, or thing. With its distinctive structure and the freedom to adopt any rhythmic pattern, odes showcase versatility. They can evoke a spectrum of emotions, ranging from solemnity to lightheartedness, while emanating deep admiration or a profound sense of wonder. In the realm of odes, poets weave their words to pay homage, creating a harmonious symphony of praise and celebration.

EXAMPLE: 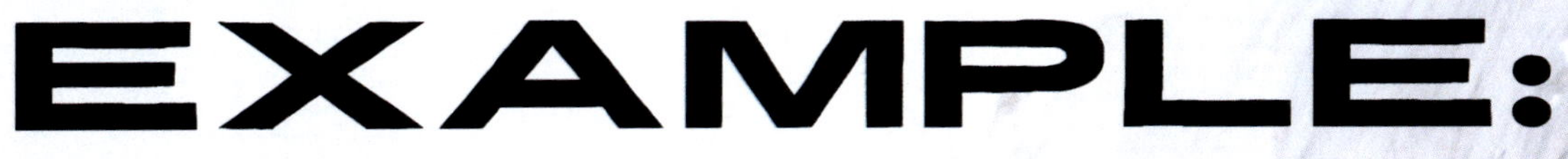

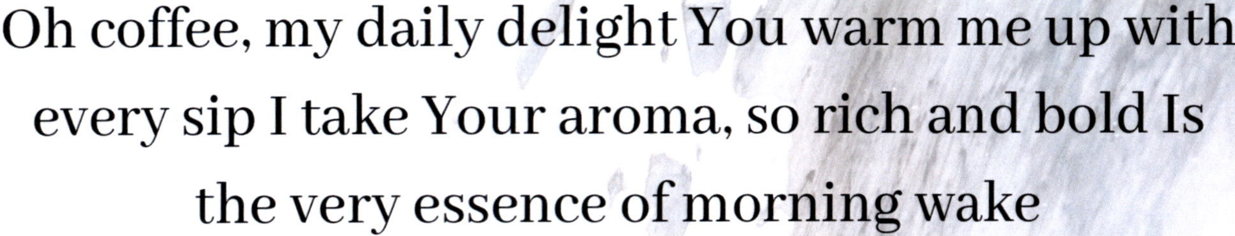

Ode to Coffee

Oh coffee, my daily delight You warm me up with
every sip I take Your aroma, so rich and bold Is
the very essence of morning wake

Your flavor, so diverse and strong Is the perfect
accompaniment to my day From espresso shots to
lattes long You never fail to brighten my way

You are the fuel that powers my mind And the
elixir that soothes my soul With each cup, I leave
my cares behind And embrace the world, whole
and whole

Oh coffee, my faithful friend You never let me
down In you, I find my happy end And my
sweetest joys abound.

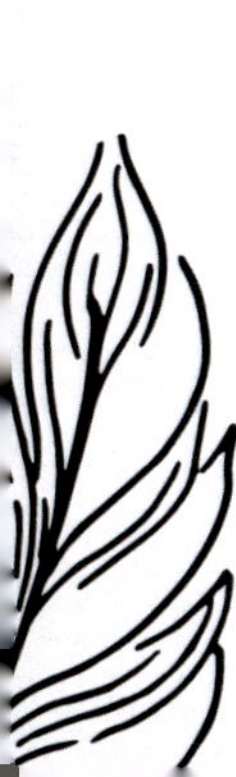

write an ode to a piece of art or literature that has impacted you

write an ode to a childhood memory or experience

write an ode to a memorable moment in your life

____

____

____

____

____

____

____

____

____

____

Date : ___________________

write an ode to your favorite food or dish

write an Ode to your closest friend or family member

Poetry is not only dream and vision; it is the skeleton architecture of our lives. It lays the foundations for a future of change, a bridge across our fears of what has never been before.

AUDRE LORDE

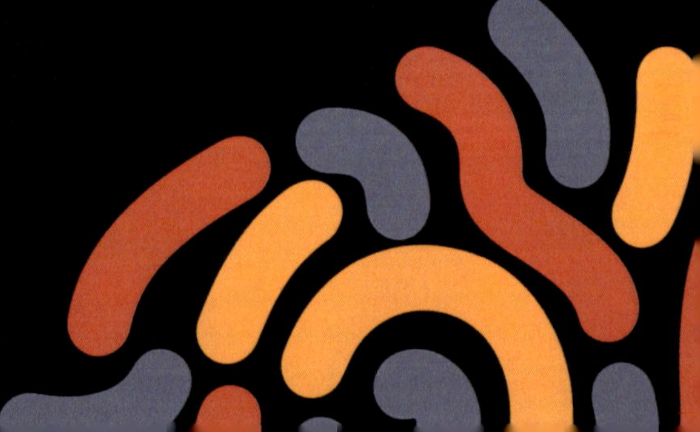

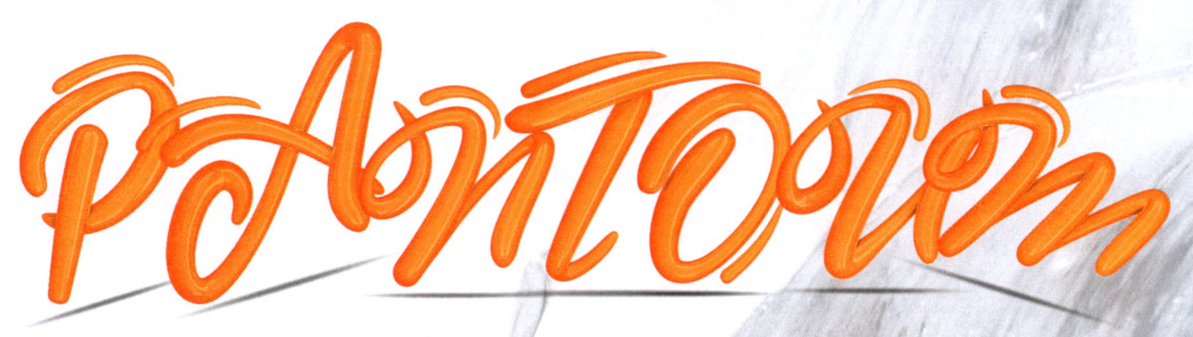

PANTOUM

A unique form of poetry characterized by its distinct pattern of repeated lines. In a pantoum, certain lines are repeated and rearranged throughout the poem, creating a captivating sense of circularity and repetition. This deliberate structure adds a mesmerizing rhythm and depth to the poem, as ideas and phrases echo and intertwine, weaving a tapestry of meaning. The repetitive nature of the pantoum enhances the thematic exploration and allows for nuanced variations and shifts in perspective, inviting the reader on a captivating journey through the interconnected threads of the poem.

EXAMPLE:

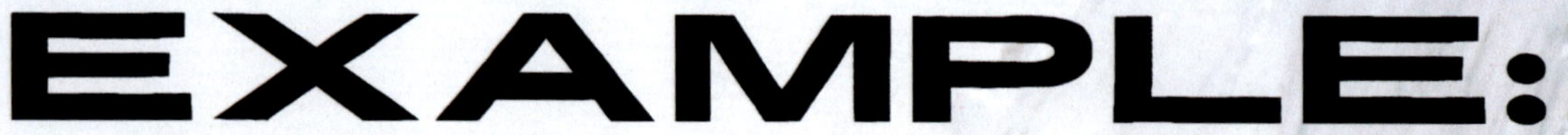

Lost in Thought

Lost in thought, I wander through the day My mind a maze of winding roads and bends My thoughts, like leaves, fall soft and gentle And I follow, wherever they may wend

My mind a maze of winding roads and bends A labyrinth of memories and dreams And I follow, wherever they may wend Through fields of green and streams that gleam

A labyrinth of memories and dreams Each one a window to my soul Through fields of green and streams that gleam My thoughts, like clouds, drift and roll

Each one a window to my soul My thoughts, like leaves, fall soft and gentle My mind a maze of winding roads and bends Lost in thought, I wander through the day.

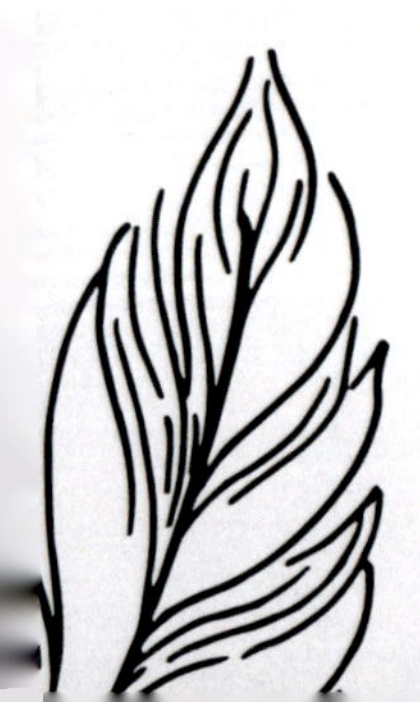

Create a pantoum about a dream you had

Write a pantoum about a place you feel most at peace.

Date : _______________

Write a pantoum about a significant event in your
life and how it made you feel.

____

____

____

____

____

____

____

____

____

____

Create a pantoum about a moment of pure joy or happiness.

Write a pantoum about a place you've never been
but dream of visiting.

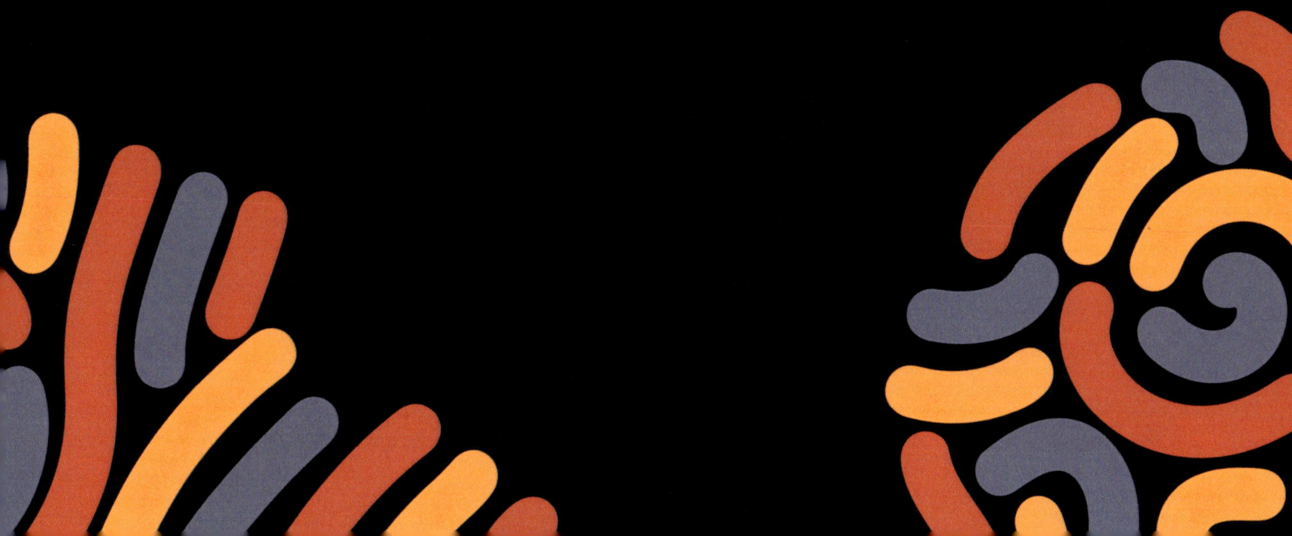

Hold fast to dreams, for if dreams die, life is a broken-winged bird that cannot fly.

LANGSTON HUGHES

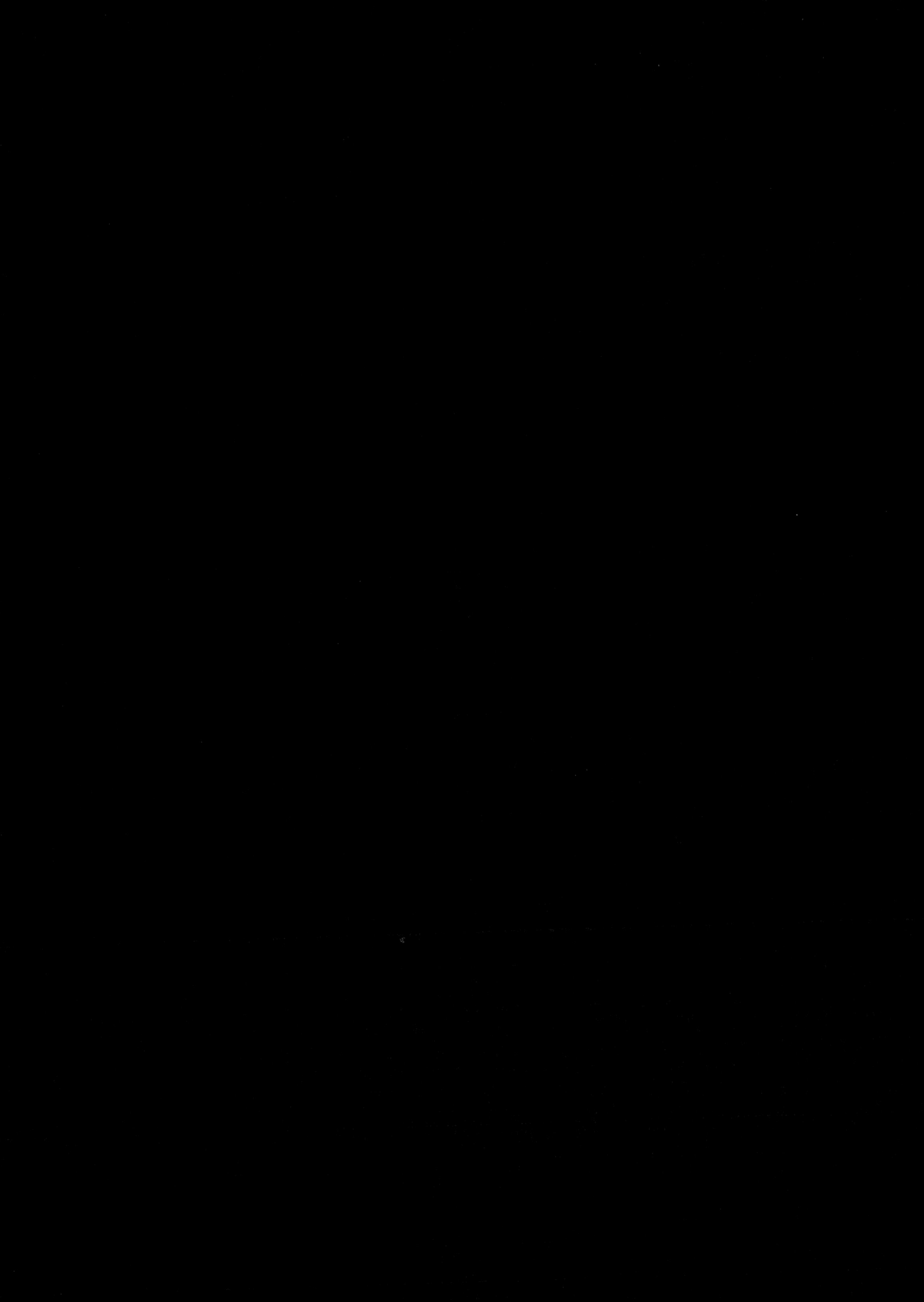

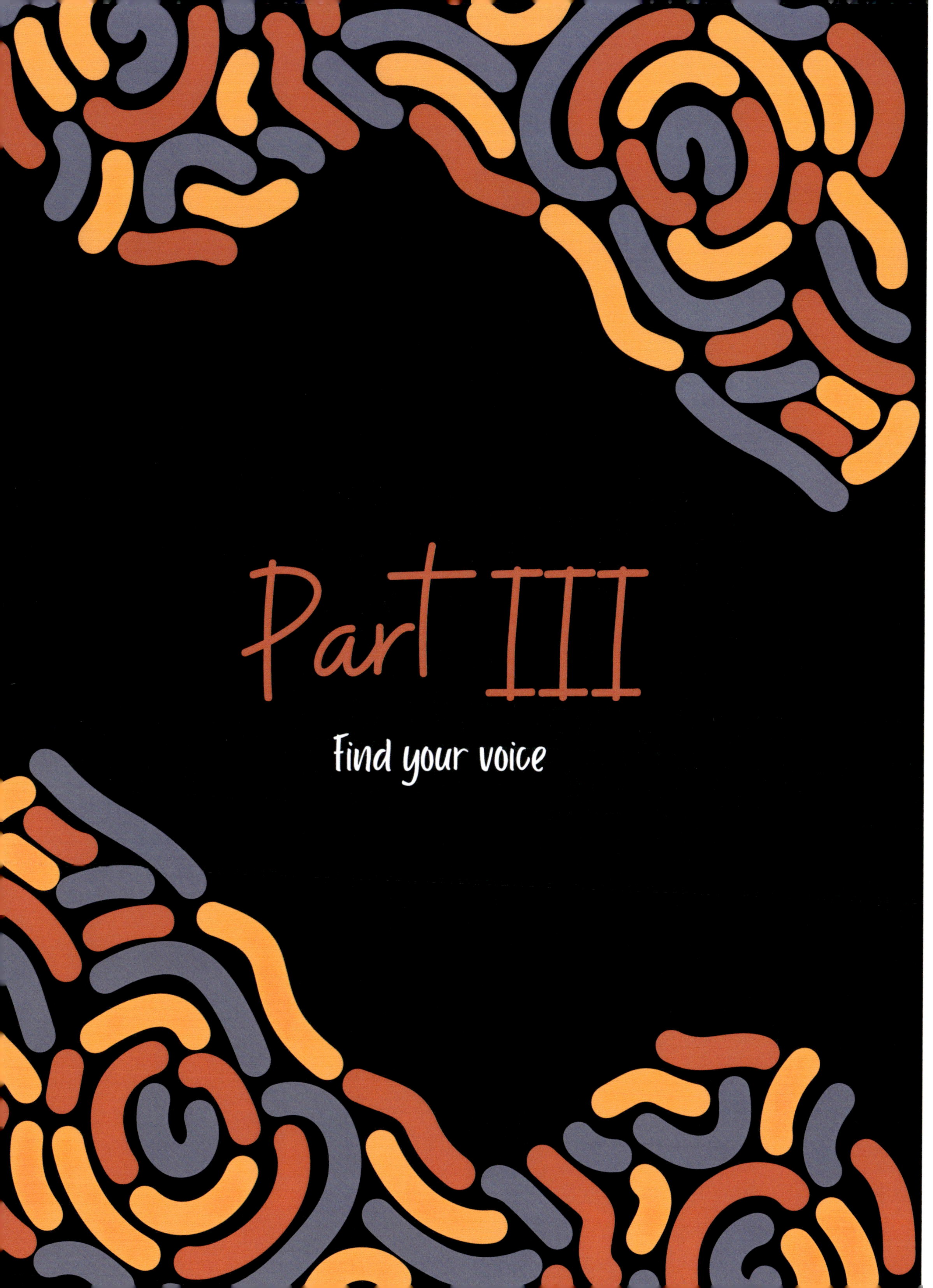

Part III
Find your voice

FREE FORM EXPRESSION

Welcome to the transformative "Find Your Voice" journal section, where you are invited to embark on a journey of self-discovery and unearth the essence of your unique voice. To embark on this path, you must embrace the profound impact of literature and introspection. By delving deep into the realms of both written words and your inner self, you will uncover the raw materials that poetry and self-expression thrive upon. This section celebrates subjectivity, honoring the richness of your interior world, and beckons you to delve within, to excavate your roots and find your true voice. It is an empowering call to action, inviting you to embrace the transformative power of self-expression and honor the depths of your being through the written word. Embrace this opportunity to embark on a profound journey of self-discovery, as you unlock the poetic treasures within and give voice to the very essence of who you are.

Date : _______________

Date :

Date : _______________

Date:

Date :

Date :

Date :

Date :

VISUALIZE

Finding your voice through visualizing is a powerful journey of self-expression. By putting pen to paper and capturing expressions through drawing, you embark on a visual exploration of your inner world. With each stroke of the pencil, you breathe life into your thoughts and emotions, allowing your true voice to emerge and speak volumes without uttering a single word.

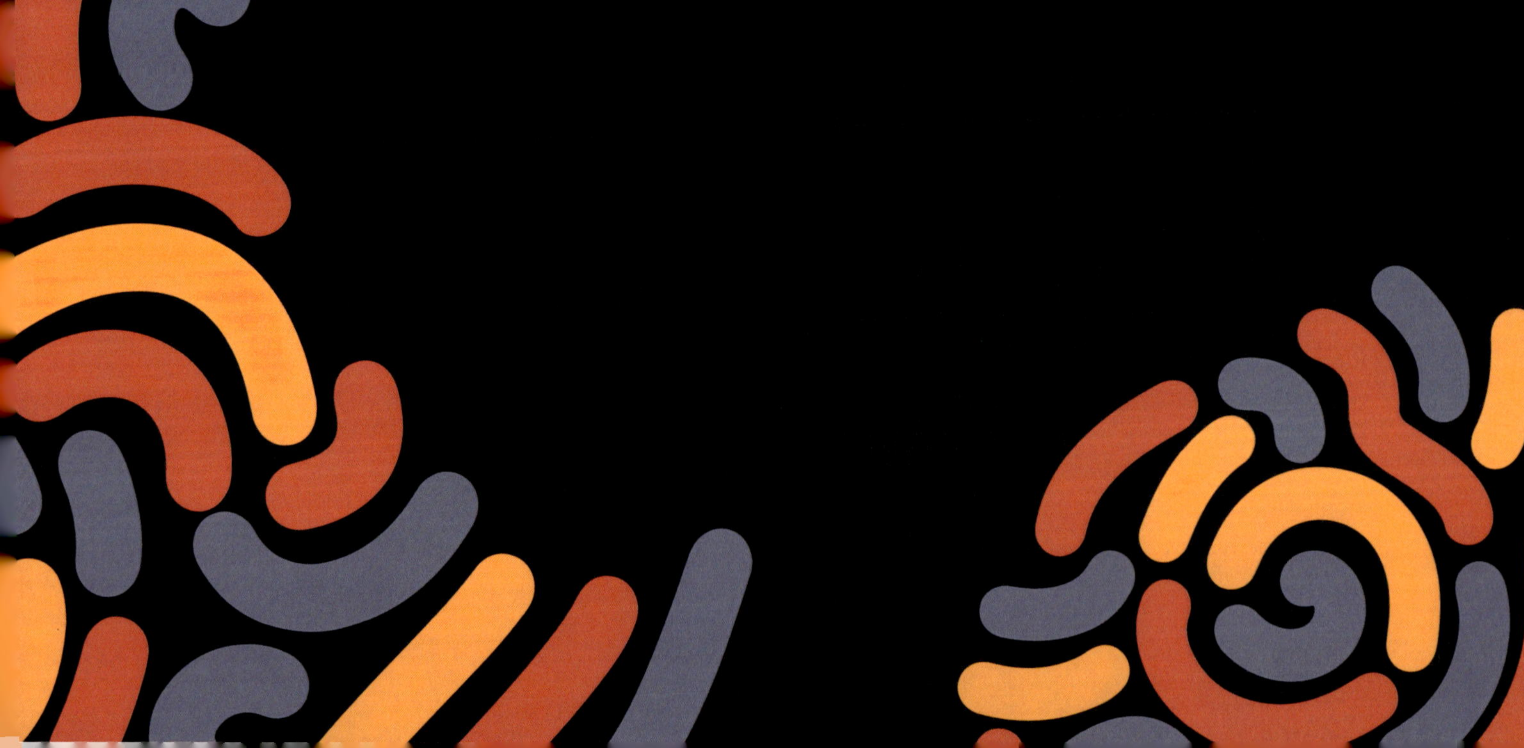

The world is before you, and you need not take it or leave it as it was when you came in.

JAMES BALDWIN

Date :

Date :

Date : _______________

Date :

Date : _______________

Date :

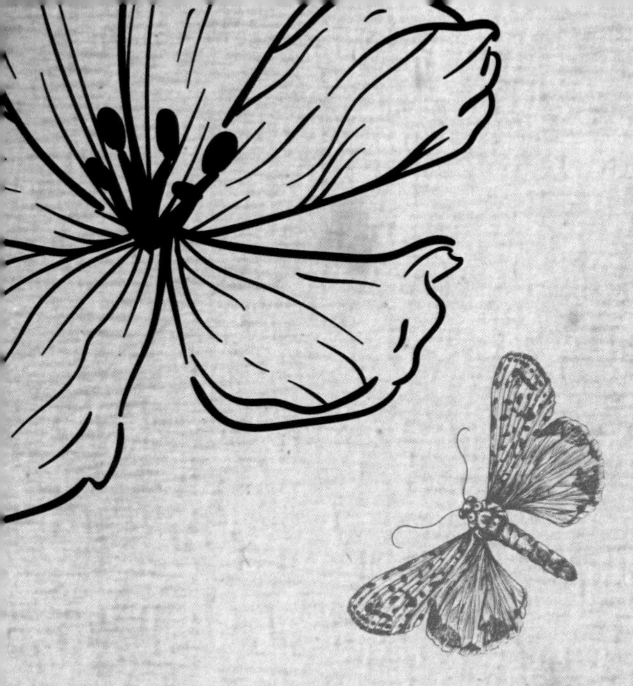

Every Breath is inspiration.
Never stop creating.

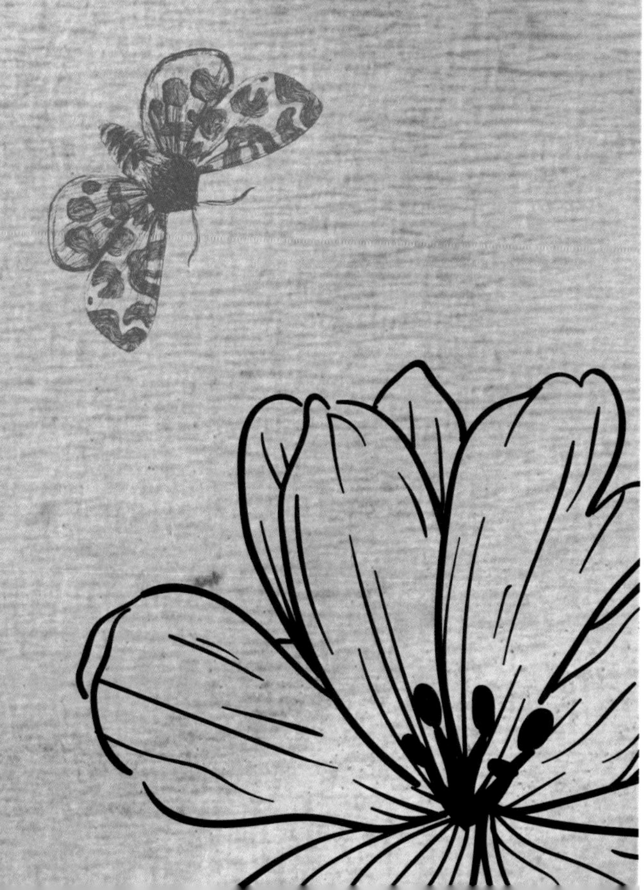

Date :

Date : ______________

Date :

Date : _______________

Date :

Date : _______________

Date :

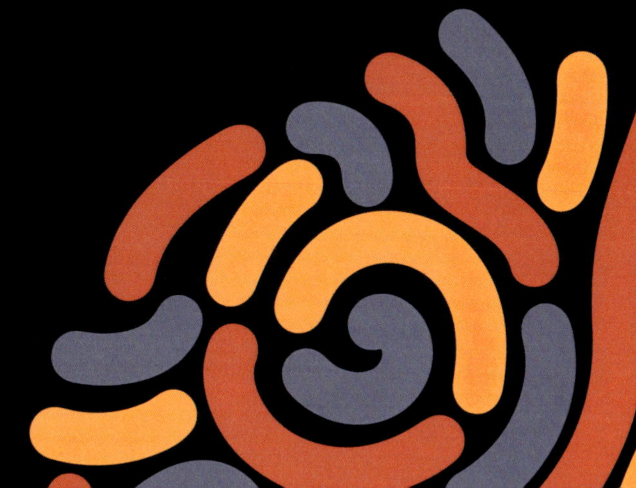

The time will come when you will hear the whales and the birds speak to you with intelligence.

ALICE WALKER

Date : _______________

Date : ________________

Date :

Date :

Date :

Date :

Date :

Date : ______________

Date :

Date : _______________

VISUALIZE

Finding your voice through visualizing is a powerful journey of self-expression. By putting pen to paper and capturing expressions through drawing, you embark on a visual exploration of your inner world. With each stroke of the pencil, you breathe life into your thoughts and emotions, allowing your true voice to emerge and speak volumes without uttering a single word.

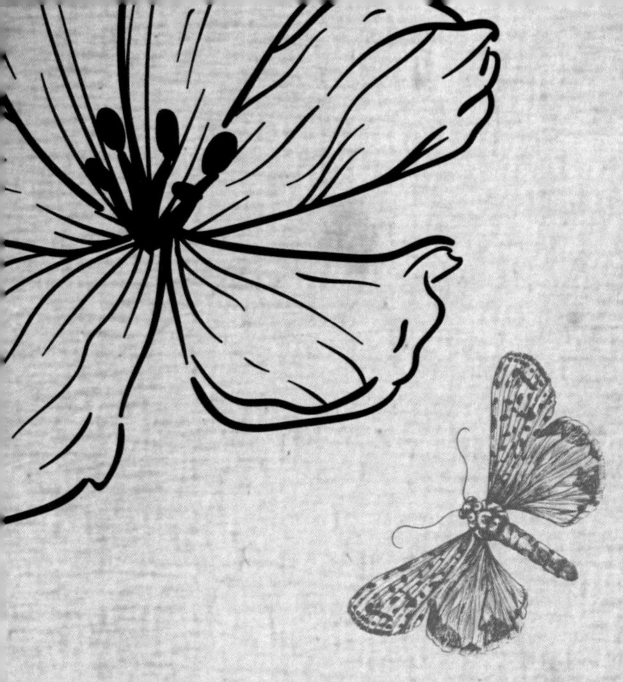

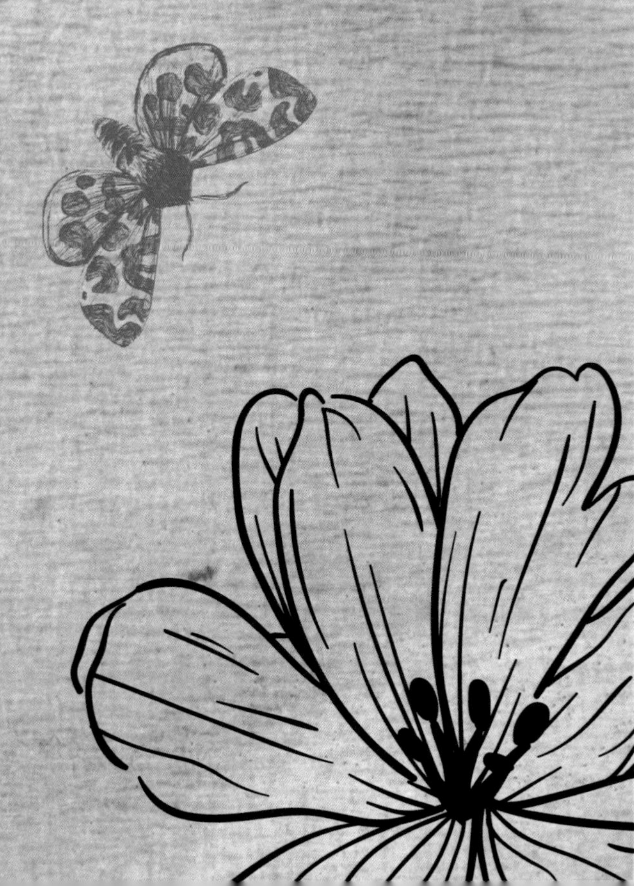

Poetry is not only dream and vision; it is the skeleton architecture of our lives

Sylvia Plath

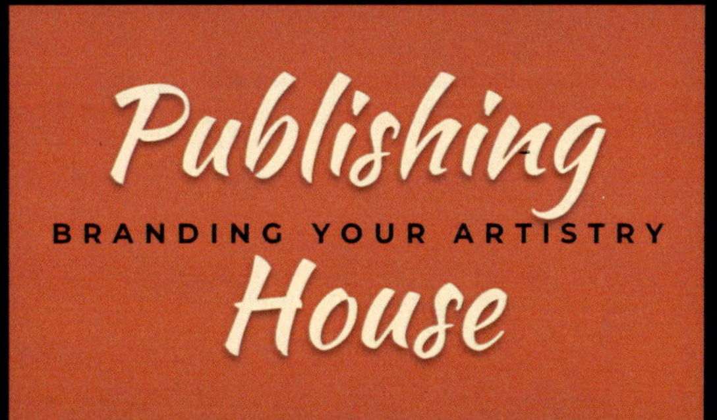

Branding Your Artistry Publishing House, a subsidiary of Branding Your Artistry LLC, extends a warm invitation to establish a lasting connection and become an integral part of our vibrant community. Embrace the opportunity to stay informed and inspired by following us on social media, @Branding_Your_Artistry, where you will find valuable branding advice and creative insights to elevate your artistic journey. For any requirements related to book publishing, editing, or design, we encourage you to reach out to us at BrandingYourArtistryLLC@gmail.com, where our dedicated team stands ready to assist you with professionalism and expertise. Join us on this empowering path of artistic fulfillment and let us empower your creative vision.

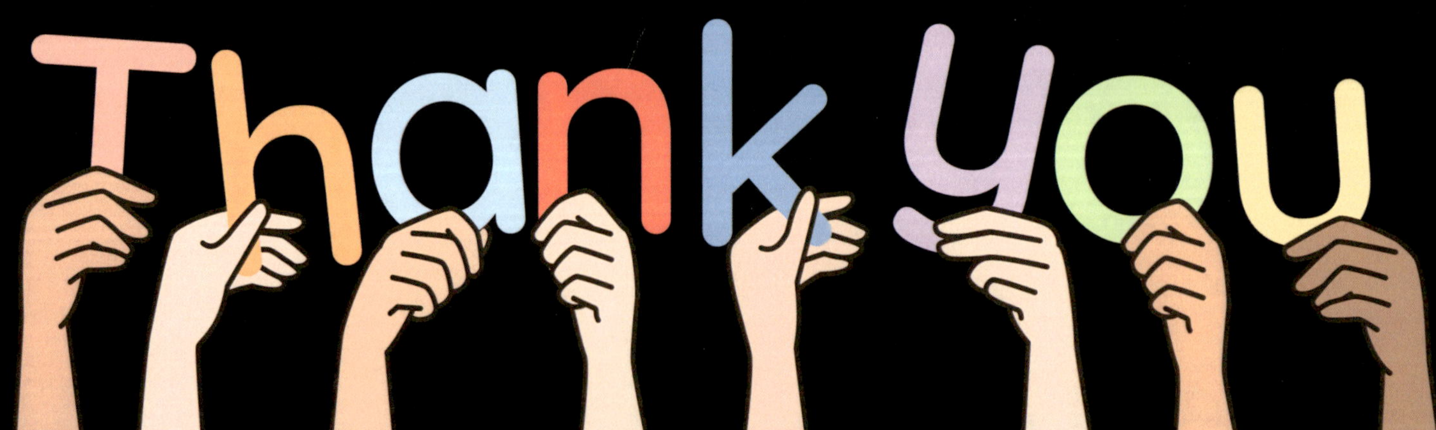

H.O.C.A
House Of Creative Artists
Thank you